Contents

Words in **bold** can be found
in the glossary.

The Tudors

The Tudors were a family who ruled England from 1485 to 1603. The Tudor period began when Henry Tudor defeated his rival, Richard III, at the Battle of Bosworth Field in 1485.

Tudor kings and queens

Henry Tudor was crowned King Henry VII. He was a strict and shrewd ruler who brought peace and prosperity to his kingdom. When he died in 1509, he was succeeded by his son, Henry VIII. The young king was very different from his father. Henry was good-looking and extravagant, a great athlete with a passion for art and music.

In this portrait of Henry VIII, the king's lavish jewellery and expensive clothes display both his wealth and power.

King Henry VIII, 1491–1547

Famously, Henry VIII had six wives. He married Catherine of Aragon in 1509. She was the mother of Mary, but despite many pregnancies she did not produce the male heir for whom Henry longed. Henry divorced her in 1533 and married Anne Boleyn, mother of Elizabeth. Henry had Anne executed in 1536 and quickly married Jane Seymour, who gave birth to a son, Edward. She died shortly afterwards. Henry's last three wives were Anne of Cleves (divorced), Catherine Howard (executed) and Catherine Parr (who outlived him).

Henry VIII had three children, Mary, Elizabeth and Edward. As Henry's only son, Edward became king at the age of nine when Henry died in 1547. But Edward's health was poor, and he died in 1553. He was succeeded by Henry's elder daughter, Mary. The last great reign of the Tudor period was that of Queen Elizabeth I, who succeeded Mary in 1558. Elizabeth did not marry, and left no heirs to the throne, so the Tudor period came to an end when she died in 1603.

Tudor people

The Tudor period was largely a time of peace when **trade** flourished, and some people became immensely wealthy. Many of the houses built by the richest and most powerful people in Tudor times still stand today (see pages 10–13). At the other end of the scale, the number of poor people rose rapidly during the period (see pages 16–17), and for these people life was often very hard.

 Montacute House in Somerset was built during the reign of Queen Elizabeth I by Sir Edward Phelips, who made his fortune as a lawyer.

Tudor style

Most people in Tudor times used materials that could be found locally to build their homes. This meant that the houses of ordinary people looked different from region to region.

House building

Transport in Tudor times was difficult and slow. The roads were bumpy and muddy, so only the wealthy could afford to have heavy building materials moved from one part of the country to another. Ordinary people made use of local materials such as stone, timber or bricks. The simplest homes were made from **cob**, a mixture of mud, straw and water. Walls made from cob were built up in layers, and then allowed to dry.

Cruck frames

Many Tudor houses had frames made from timber, often oak. The simplest type of timber frame was the **cruck frame**, which was an upside-down V shape held together by long pieces of wood called **rafters**. The roof was often covered with thatch, while the walls were built from whatever material was at hand – clay, turf or stone, for example.

Some Tudor houses had beautifully decorated chimney pots. These chimney pots are made from bricks.

Box frames

A more expensive style of timber frame was the **box frame**. The timbers were pinned together with wooden pegs to make a rectangular frame with a triangular roof on top. Short pieces of timber, called studs, were fixed into the frame to make it stronger. The spaces between the studs were filled in to make the walls. Builders used local materials for these wall fillings. In some places, brick or clay mixed with stone were used. In other places, the spaces were filled with thin branches that were woven together to make a mesh, called a **wattle**. This was covered with a mixture of clay or mud and straw, called **daub**.

A Tudor object

The timber frame of a house was often painted with black tar to protect it, and the daub was painted white. The pattern of black-and-white can still be seen on many Tudor buildings today, and this style of housing has been much copied since Tudor times.

Little Moreton Hall in Cheshire is a timber-framed house that was built for the Moreton family mainly during the Tudor period. The timber frame was designed to make attractive patterns.

Royal palaces

By the time of his death in 1547, King Henry VIII had no less than 60 royal houses and palaces. One of his favourites was Hampton Court Palace, which originally belonged to his chief minister, Cardinal Thomas Wolsey.

⬆ The Great Hall in Hampton Court Palace was built by Henry VIII for banquets and entertainment.

Hampton Court Palace

Hampton Court lies on the River Thames west of London. Thomas Wolsey acquired the house in 1514 and immediately began work to turn it into a magnificent palace. During the 1520s, Wolsey fell out of favour with Henry VIII, and the king forced Wolsey to give him Hampton Court. Wolsey died in 1529, and Henry started more building work at the palace.

By the time this work was finished in 1540, the palace had kitchens that were big enough to provide food for 600 people twice a day, tennis courts and bowling alleys, and a large communal lavatory where 28 people could sit at the same time!

Written at the time

Paul Hentzner, a German nobleman, described the splendours of Hampton Court Palace in 1598:

'Hampton Court, a Royal Palace, magnificently built with brick by Cardinal Wolsey in ostentation of [to show off] his wealth, where he enclosed five very ample courts, consisting of noble edifices [structures] in very beautiful work... The chief area is paved with square stone; in its centre is a fountain that throws up water, covered with a gilt crown, on the top of which is a statue of Justice, supported by columns of black and white marble.'

Nonsuch Palace

Henry VIII and his household moved from one palace to the next throughout the year. The king was usually attended by around 1,000 people, so moving the royal household was a major undertaking! Henry loved to go hunting, and in 1538 he decided to build a new palace on his hunting estate in Surrey. He brought craftworkers from Europe to work on the decorations and furnishings for his splendid palace, which was named Nonsuch. Unfortunately, the palace was demolished in 1682, and only a few pictures remain to show us how magnificent it was.

⬇ The walls of Nonsuch Palace were highly decorated with human and animal figures.

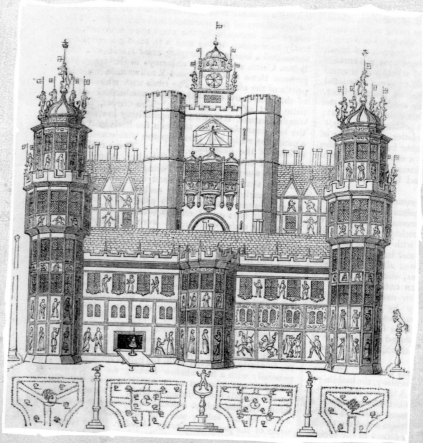

Built to impress

Henry VIII built palaces to show off his immense wealth and power. He spent more than £62,000 (the equivalent of £18 million today) on Hampton Court Palace.

Royal progresses

Henry's daughter, Queen Elizabeth I, did not spend such vast sums on building work. She did, however, expect her wealthy **courtiers** to lavish their money on impressive buildings. Every year, the queen went on a journey around England, called a royal progress. She stayed in her own palaces, including Nonsuch, and in the houses of her courtiers, who all tried to outdo each other to provide the most lavish accommodation and entertainment for their queen.

Prodigy houses

The grand country houses built by wealthy landowners during Tudor times are often called **prodigy houses**, because of their large size and sumptuous decoration. There are many examples that still stand today, including Burghley House in Lincolnshire, Longleat and Montacute House (see page 7), both in Somerset, and Hardwick Hall in Derbyshire.

Queen Elizabeth I passes in front of Nonsuch Palace during one of her royal progresses. This drawing dates from 1568.

Burghley was built by William Cecil, Elizabeth's chief and most trusted adviser. Like many prodigy houses, Burghley was designed in the shape of an E, in honour of Elizabeth.

Hardwick Hall was built for the Countess of Shrewsbury. A **stonemason** and **architect** called Robert Smythson designed the house that displayed its owner's wealth and power for everyone to see. Glass was an expensive luxury in Elizabethan England, but Hardwick had so many huge windows that people said of it, 'Hardwick Hall – more glass than wall'.

Bess of Hardwick had her initials (ES for Elizabeth Shrewsbury) carved out of the stone parapets that ran around the edge of the roof of her grand new house at Hardwick.

Bess of Hardwick, 1527–1608

Elizabeth, Countess of Shrewsbury, was better known as Bess of Hardwick. She was born at Hardwick in 1527, and rose to power and wealth through her four marriages, becoming the second most powerful woman in Elizabethan England after the queen. During her second marriage, to William Cavendish, she built a grand house at Chatsworth in Derbyshire. Bess's fourth marriage was not a happy one. In the 1580s, Bess left Chatsworth and returned to Hardwick, where she set about building a new house for herself.

Townhouses

In Tudor times, most people in England lived in small villages in the countryside. The biggest city was London, which had a population of more than 250,000 by 1600. Other important Tudor towns were Bristol, Norwich, York and Exeter.

This detail from an engraving of London by the Dutch artist Claes Jansz Visscher was made some years after the death of Elizabeth I, but it shows the city as it looked during late Tudor times.

Dirty and smelly

Many streets in Tudor towns were not paved and quickly turned to mud when it rained. Tudor towns were very dirty and smelly places! People threw all their rubbish on to the streets, including toilet waste. Some streets had open **sewers** that ran into the nearest stream or river. People got clean (or nearly clean) water for washing and cooking from wells and pumps, or from water sellers who carried the water in carriers on their backs.

The dirty conditions meant that rats and other **vermin** were common, and that outbreaks of disease such as the **plague** were frequent. In 1563, around 20,000 people died when the plague swept across London.

Tradesmen and merchants

In Tudor towns, tradesmen often lived and worked in the same street. In Tudor Bristol, the **cutlers** (people who make tools for cutting) and **armourers** (people who make arms and armour) traded on a street called Knifesmith Street. In York, the Shambles was where butchers and slaughterhouses were found ('shambles' is an old word for a place from which meat is sold).

Many merchants in Tudor times became very rich, making their fortunes through the sale of goods such as wool, cloth or coal. Wealthy merchants often built comfortable townhouses for themselves, some of which still stand today.

This lane in Canterbury, near the cathedral gate, gives us an idea of what a typical street looked like in Tudor times.

A Tudor object

Tudor townhouses were often built with overhanging upper storeys. The part that hung out over the street was called the **jetty**. This design meant that the ground floors took up less space than the upper floors. It also meant that streets were often very dark, because the overhanging buildings blocked out the light above. You can still see examples of Tudor jettied townhouses in many cities and towns in England.

The poor

The Tudor period was a time when the **population** grew rapidly. Unfortunately, the number of jobs did not increase as quickly, which meant that many people could not find work.

Workhouses and almshouses

Poverty and unemployment were huge problems throughout the period. Poor families suffered particularly during times of bad harvests, when the price of food rose. People were not allowed to leave their **parishes** to go looking for work. Those that did risked being branded as vagrants or vagabonds, and if they were caught they could be whipped and sent back home.

In 1550, parliament passed a law to establish a workhouse in every parish. In exchange for food and shelter in the workhouse, poor people were expected to work for no wages. The wealthy people of a parish were expected to give help, called **alms**, to look after the poor in their area. Wealthy people also gave money for **almshouses** – communities in which the elderly were cared for.

These almshouses are part of the Hospital of St Cross in Winchester.

Homes for the poor

Homes for poor people were usually simple one-storey houses with one or two rooms. Chimneys were a luxury reserved for the houses of the rich. Most people had a hole in the roof to let out smoke, making the inside of the house very smoky. Glass for the windows was also a luxury. The poor used strips of linen that were soaked in **linseed oil** to cover the windows and keep out draughts.

The growth in the cloth trade, which made many merchants rich (see page 15), reduced the number of jobs in the countryside even further. Many farmers stopped growing crops and instead put sheep on their land, to provide wool for the cloth trade. Many farm labourers lost both their jobs and their homes, and large numbers of them headed for the towns and cities to try to start new lives.

⬆ This painting by the Dutch artist Hieronymus Bosch shows a vagabond being turned away from an inn.

Written at the time

William Harrison was an English clergyman. He described the plight of the poor in Holinshed's *Chronicles* of 1577:

'For the first two sorts (that is to say, the poor by impotence [age or illness] and poor by casualty [accident], which are the true poor indeed...), there is order taken throughout every parish in the realm that weekly collection shall be made for their help and sustention [sustainment] — to the end they shall not scatter abroad, and, by begging here and there, annoy both town and country.'

Running the home

The work of running a home was called 'housewifery'. Tudor housewives did all the cooking, cleaning and childcare, as well as other jobs such as feeding the animals or looking after the bees.

Practical skills

Tudor women had a huge range of practical skills. Even wealthy women were brought up to be working housewives, often running large estates with the help of their servants. Girls were taught how to cook and some medical skills – what herbs to use to keep their families in good health. Women were also responsible for making the clothes worn by all the members of their families.

A Tudor object

Bees provide both beeswax and honey. In Tudor times, the wax was used to make high-quality candles, while the honey was used as a sweetener. Honey was also used in some medicines, to make polish, and to make various drinks. The weakest of these alcoholic drinks was called mead, while the strongest version – which was favoured by Elizabeth I – was called metheglin.

The beehive shown in this illustration, called a skep, was made from tightly bound coils of straw. The bees built their honeycomb inside it.

Some women took on paid work, too. It was common for jobs such as the spinning of wool to be done in people's homes (known as 'piecework'). Merchants delivered the raw wool, than collected it once it had been washed, combed out and spun into woollen thread, ready for weaving. At busy times in the countryside, such as harvest, women were also expected to work with their menfolk in the fields.

Looking after animals

Villages in the countryside did not have shops – people who could afford it kept a few animals on **common land**, and grew a few crops. A housewife might start her day by milking the family's cow. The milk was used for drinking and for making butter and cheese in the dairy. Other animals often included hens and geese (kept for their eggs and meat) and, pigs and bees. Housewives were expected to tend their gardens, too (see pages 26–27).

This coloured woodcut shows a maid milking a cow. The milk from both cows and sheep was made into butter and cheese.

Clean and healthy

Washing and cleaning were part of a housewife's everyday chores. Very few houses had running water, so before any washing could begin the first job was to collect fresh water from the nearest well or pump.

Cleaning and washing

It was hard work to keep a Tudor home clean. Walls made from wattle and daub housed all manner of insects, and most houses had earth floors that were often dusty and dirty. Wealthy people, however, could afford stone floors that could be scrubbed clean. Utensils for eating and cooking were commonly made from wood. They were **scoured** with sand and hot water to clean them. Wealthy people had plates and cups made from **pewter**, which was easier to keep clean.

Washing clothes and household linen was always a woman's job. Many housewives who could afford it employed washerwomen to do this heavy work for them. Linen and clothes were washed in big wooden tubs, then spread out on the ground or on small bushes to dry.

This water pump is made of cast iron. People in Tudor times collected fresh water from their nearest pump.

Personal hygiene

People in Tudor times kept themselves as clean as they could. Henry VIII had magnificent bathrooms in his palaces, but, for most ordinary people, having a bath meant fetching and heating the water, then filling a large wooden tub.

For teeth cleaning, people used twigs, pieces of wet linen, and a mixture of vinegar, wine and honey, which was rubbed onto the teeth. However, many people didn't clean their teeth at all, and toothache was a common ailment.

Tudor toilets were known as garderobes or jakes. There was often a separate pot for the urine, which was saved and used in a mixture to **bleach** linen.

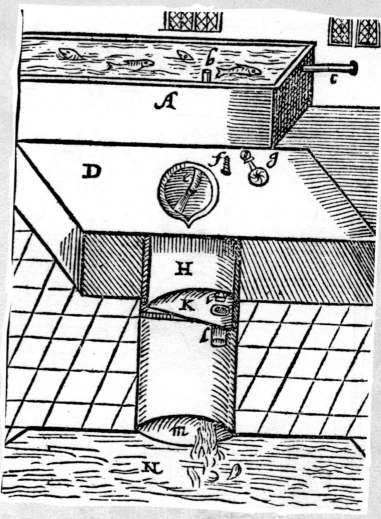

In the 1590s, Sir John Harington invented the flush toilet, illustrated here. He had a version installed at his house near Bath, but his idea did not catch on in Tudor England.

Written at the time

The Tudors used a wide range of herbs and plants to treat illness. Garlic was considered to be a powerful medicine, and was often called the 'poor man's physic' [medicine]. This description of the powers of garlic comes from *The Gardener's Labyrinth* (1577):

'Garlike putteth away inward swellings, openeth impostumes [abscesses], killeth lice and nits of the head, moveth urine, helpeth toothach proceeding from a cold cause.'

Food and drink

For most people in Tudor times, food was made from whatever ingredients were available locally. Only the very wealthy could afford to buy exotic foods from abroad, such as oranges or lemons.

Pottage and bread

The basic foods that were eaten everyday by the vast majority of the population in Tudor England were **pottage** and bread. Pottage was a kind of soup or porridge made from seasonal vegetables and a grain such as oats or barley. For most poor people, meat was a luxury that was reserved for special occasions only. Tudor bread was much heavier and denser than bread today, and people ate large amounts of it to fill themselves up.

Meat

Most families who could afford it kept a pig for its meat. When the pig was killed, the meat was salted or smoked to preserve it for as long as possible. Wealthy people, however, had enough animals to provide fresh meat all year round – or they could buy meat from the butchers' shops in towns. Henry VIII and his courtiers ate huge amounts of meat – it has been estimated that 80 per cent of the king's diet was made up of various types of meat.

A selection of Tudor knives. Knives were used to cut and eat food. Spoons were rarer and highly prized, and forks were virtually unknown in most of Europe until the 1700s.

Food for a fine meal is prepared in a kitchen in Tudor times.

Fish

In Tudor times, there were laws about what people were allowed to eat, and when. On Fridays and Saturdays, and during the fasting times of Lent (before Easter) and Advent (before Christmas), people ate fish instead of meat. Fresh fish was a luxury, so most people ate stockfish, a kind of hard, dried fish (often cod).

Ale and wine

Most people in Tudor times avoided drinking water because it was almost always polluted and it made them ill. The most common drink was ale, which was brewed from barley and which could be flavoured with almost anything. Wealthy people also drank wine, which was imported from abroad.

A Tudor object

This tankard was made for the Parr family, and the coat of arms on the lid is that of Sir William Parr, who was uncle to Henry VIII's sixth wife, Catherine (see page 6). Only the wealthiest people could afford such luxurious items.

A glass and silver tankard from the 1540s.

Furniture

Poor people in Tudor times had very little furniture in their homes. The houses of the wealthy, however, became far more comfortable during this period.

Floors and walls

Floors were usually covered with straw or rushes, which, if not changed regularly, quickly became dirty and smelly. In wealthy homes, herbs were often added to try to keep the floor covering sweet-smelling. In houses of the well-to-do, oak was used to line the walls of **parlours** and bedrooms. This **panelling** helped to keep the rooms warm. Very wealthy people also hung tapestries, carpets or painted cloths on their walls.

⬆ Wood-panelled walls in the Great Chamber in Sutton House in Hackney, London.

Written at the time

William Harrison described how wall hangings or panelling were used in the houses of the wealthy in *A Description of Elizabethan England*, 1577:

'The walls of our houses on the inner sides ... be either hanged with tapestry ... or painted cloths, wherein either divers histories, or herbs, beasts, knots [patterns], and such like are stained, or else they are ceiled with oak of our own, ... whereby the rooms are not a little commended, made warm, and much more close than otherwise they would be.'

Types of furniture

For most poor people, furniture was a luxury. They were lucky to have a table, stools or benches to sit on, a wooden chest for storing clothes or linen, and mattresses stuffed with straw. In richer households, fine furniture was treasured and passed down from one generation to the next. Most Tudor furniture was made from oak, and it was often beautifully carved. People usually sat on stools – chairs were unusual and expensive. Presses (large wardrobes) were used to store clothes. The most wealthy had four-poster beds, with curtains that could be drawn to keep out draughts.

The Great Bed of Ware was probably made in the 1590s for an inn at Ware, Hertfordshire. It is three metres wide – about twice the size of a normal bed of this period.

Lighting

Rooms were lit with candles. The most expensive were those made from beeswax. Other candles were made from animal fat (tallow), but they gave off an unpleasant smell as they were burned. For those who could not afford candles at all, rushes dipped in animal fat provided a little light.

Gardens

Gardening was very popular in Tudor times. People grew vegetables and fruit to eat. They also became very interested in the new plants that were introduced from abroad.

Vegetables and fruits

Housewives used their gardens to feed their families. They planted vegetables such as onions, leeks, garlic and cabbages. Herbs such as sage, thyme, lavender, rosemary, borage and parsley were used for cooking and as medicines. Many gardens had small orchards where apple, plum and pear trees were grown. New varieties of fruit, including peaches and apricots, also became popular among the wealthy.

Gardens for show

Like prodigy houses, the gardens of wealthy people were designed to impress. The garden at Theobalds, one of William Cecil's houses (see page 13), had fountains, mazes and elaborate knot gardens.

← Fruit was usually cooked rather than eaten fresh in Tudor times, as doctors thought that raw food caused illness.

Knot gardens were gardens laid out with low hedges that created patterns when seen from above. One of Cecil's knot gardens was in the shape of Henry VIII's coat of arms in order to honour the king.

Many people had a great interest in the new varieties of plants that were being brought from the Americas and from Europe. Flowers such as tulips were highly prized for their colour, while a few people experimented with growing new fruits and vegetables such as the tomato and potato, both brought over from the Americas.

⇧ Tudor House in Southampton has a beautiful knot garden.

Written at the time

William Harrison commented on the new types of plants appearing in England's gardens and orchards:

'And even as it fareth with our gardens, so doth it with our orchards, which were never furnished with so good fruit nor with such variety as at this present. For, beside that we have most delicate apples, plums, pears, walnuts, filberts [hazels], etc., and those of sundry sorts, planted within forty years past, ... so have we no less store of strange fruit, as apricots, almonds, peaches, figs, ... in noblemen's orchards. I have seen capers, oranges, and lemons, and heard of wild olives growing here, beside other strange trees, brought from far, whose names I know not.'

Timeline

1485	Battle of Bosworth Field and death of Richard III. Beginning of the Tudor era when Henry VII becomes king.
1492	Christopher Columbus sails to the Americas.
1509	Death of Henry VII; Henry VIII succeeds to the throne and marries Catherine of Aragon.
1514	Cardinal Thomas Wolsey begins work at Hampton Court.
1529	Henry VIII starts building work at Hampton Court.
1533	Henry VIII marries Anne Boleyn.
1536	Death of Catherine of Aragon; execution of Anne Boleyn; Henry VIII marries Jane Seymour.
1536-40	Henry VIII closes down the monasteries in England.
1537	Birth of Prince Edward (later Edward VI); death of Jane Seymour.
1540	Henry VIII marries and divorces Anne of Cleves; marries Catherine Howard.
1547	Death of Henry VIII; Edward VI succeeds to the throne.
1553	Death of Edward VI; Lady Jane Grey becomes queen for nine days; Mary I succeeds to the throne.
1554	Mary I marries King Philip II of Spain.
1558	Mary I dies; Elizabeth I succeeds to the throne.
1568	Mary Queen of Scots flees to England.
1587	Execution of Mary Queen of Scots.
	Completion of Burghley House.
1588	Defeat of the Spanish Armada.
1597	Bess of Hardwick moves ito Hardwick Hall.
1603	Death of Queen Elizabeth I and the end of the Tudor era.

Glossary

alms gifts of money, food or clothing to help the poor

almshouse a house built with money from wealthy people or a charity for the care of the old or the poor

architect a person who designs a building

armourer a metalworker who makes arms and armour

bleach a substance that makes materials white

box frame a frame made up of vertical and horizontal supports for a building

cob a mixture of mud, straw and water that is used to make walls

common land an area of land that is for use by the public

courtier a person who attends the court of a king or queen

cruck frame a timber frame for a building that is an upside-down V shape held together by long pieces of wood

cutler a metalworker who makes tools for cutting

daub a mixture of clay or mud and straw used to plaster walls

jetty in a Tudor building, the part that juts out to support an overhanging upper storey

linseed oil oil made from flax

panelling wide, thin sheets of wood used to line the walls of a room

parishes the geographical areas around churches that are under the care of particular vicars

parlour an old-fashioned word for a sitting room

pewter a metal that is made from a mixture of tin and copper

plague a very infectious disease that is passed to people by the bites of infected fleas

population the number of people in a country

pottage in Tudor times, a kind of soup or porridge, usually made from vegetables and grains

prodigy house the name given to various houses built during the Tudor period of their large size and sumptuous decoration

rafter a beam that supports a ceiling or a roof

scour to scrub hard, often with a rough material

sewer a drain that carries dirty water

stonemason someone who carves and works with stone

trade the exchange of goods or produce for money, or for other goods

vermin small animals such as rats or fleas that can carry disease and are difficult to control

wattle thin branches that are woven together to make a mesh, often used in building

Index

Resources

History in Art: Tudor England Nicola Barber, Raintree, 2005

People in the Past: Tudor Rich and Poor Haydn Middleton, Heinemann, 2004

Who Was Henry VIII? Kay Barnham, Wayland 2007

http://www.nettlesworth.durham.sch.uk/time/tudors.html
Lots of fun information about the Tudors.

http://www.woodlands-junior.kent.sch.uk/Homework/Tudors.html
A homework help site from Woodlands Junior School.

First published in 2009 by Wayland

Copyright © Wayland 2009

Wayland
338 Euston Road
London NW1 3BH

Wayland Australia
Level 17/207 Kent Street
Sydney NSW 2000

Senior Editor: Claire Shanahan
Designer: Jane Hawkins
Picture Researcher: Kathy Lockley

British Library Cataloguing in Publication Data
Barber, Nicola
Homes. - (Tudor life)
1. Dwellings - England - History - 16th century - Juvenile
literature 2. Housing - England - History - 16th century -
Juvenile literature 3. England - Social life and customs -
16th century - Juvenile literature 4. England - Social
conditions - 16th century - Juvenile literature
I. Title
392.3'3'0942'09031

ISBN 978 0 7502 5754 1

Picture acknowledgements Mandy Barrow/www.woodlands-junior.
kent.sch.uk: 20, Bettmann/Corbis: 11, Chris Bland; Eye
Ubiquitous/Corbis: 7, Eric Crichton/Corbis: 13, Paul Heinrich/
Alamy: 16, c.INTERFOTO Pressebildargentur/Alamy: COVER
(Main), 23T, Mark Fiennes/Bridgeman Art Library, London: 27,
The Gallery Collection/Corbis: 4, 14, 18, Pawel Libera/Corbis: 10,
Lordprice Collection/Alamy: 8, 21, 28, Museum Boymans van
Beuningen, Rotterdam, The Netherlands/Bridgeman Art Library,
London: 17, Museum of London: COVER (inset), 23B, Museum
of London/Bridgeman Art Library, London: 5, 22, National Trust ,
Photographic Library/Geoffrey Frosh/Bridgeman Art Library, London: 24,
National University Library, Prague, Czech Republic/Giraudon/Bridgeman Art Library, London: 26
Clay Perry/Corbis: Titlepage, 9, Private Collection/Archives Charmet/Bridgeman Art Library, London: 19,
Brian Seed/Alamy: 12, Total London/Alamy: 8, Victoria & Albert Museum, Sally Chappell/The Art Archive:
25, Windsor Castle/The Art Archive: 6, Bo Zaunders/Corbis: 15

Printed in China

Wayland is a division of Hachette Children's Books, an Hachette UK company.
www.hachettelivre.co.uk

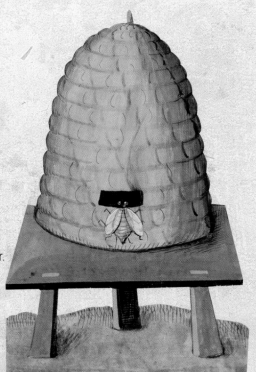

Tudor Life

HOMES

Nicola Barber

WAYLAND